£3.50

FROM CENT

Also available from Oxford:

Blood & Family (Oxford Poets), 1988
The New Oxford Book of Irish Verse (Oxford Paperbacks), 1989
The Táin (Oxford Paperbacks), 1970

FROM CENTRE CITY

Thomas Kinsella

Oxford   New York

OXFORD UNIVERSITY PRESS

1994

Oxford University Press, Walton Street, Oxford OX2 6DP

Oxford New York Toronto
Delhi Bombay Calcutta Madras Karachi
Petaling Jaya Singapore Hong Kong Tokyo
Nairobi Dar es Salaam Cape Town
Melbourne Auckland
and associated companies in
Berlin Ibadan

Oxford is a trade mark of Oxford University Press

This edition first published in Oxford Poets 1994
as an Oxford University Press paperback

The sections in this book were first published in
Dublin in limited editions as Peppercanister books:
13 One Fond Embrace; 14 Personal Places;
15 Poems from Centre City; 16 Madonna;
17 Open Court.

British Library Cataloguing in Publication Data
Data available

Library of Congress Cataloging in Publication Data
Kinsella, Thomas.
From centre city / Thomas Kinsella.
p.   cm.
I. Title.
PR6021.I35F76   1994   821'.914—dc20   93-14470
ISBN 0-19-282272-1

Typeset by J&L Composition Ltd, Filey, North Yorkshire
Printed in Hong Kong

CONTENTS

One Fond Embrace

Enough
is enough:
poring over that organic pot.

I knuckled my eyes. Their drying jellies
answered with speckles and images.
I leaned back and stretched

and embraced all
this hearth and home
echoing with the ghosts

of prides and joys,
bicycles and holy terrors,
our grown and scattered loves.

And all this place
where, it occurs to me,
I never want to be anywhere else.

Where the elements conspire.
Which is not to say
serenity and the interplay of friends

but the brick walls
of this sagging district, against which
it alerts me to knock my head.

With a scruffy nineteenth-century
history of half-finished
colonials and upstarts. Still with us.

Catholic Action next door:
the double look
over the half curtain;

social workers herding their problems
in off the street
with snooker cues and rosary beads;

Knights of Mercedes and the naked bulb
parked at large along both paths
in witness that the poor are being given a party.

With a half charm,
half gracious, spacious,
and a miscellaneous vigour.

Sniffed at. Our neighbourhood developer
thinking big in his soiled crombie.
The rodent element bidding out.

Invisible speculators, urinal architects,
and the Corporation flourishing their documents
in potent compliant dance

—planners of the wiped slate
labouring painstaking over a bungled city
to turn it into a zoo:

Southward from Fatima Mansions
into the foothills,
to where the transplanted can trudge

from Bridget's Terrace and Kennedy's Villas
via Woodbine Crescent and Cherryfield Heights
to Shangri-La for a bottle of milk;

Northward past our twinned
experimental concrete piss-towers
for the underprivileged;

and at the heart, where the river runs
through Viking ghosts at every tide
by a set of shadow structures

that our city fathers, fumbling in their shadow budget,
beheld in vision for a while,
pulverising until the cash failed,

laying flat an enduring monument to themselves,
an office car park sunk deep in history.
May their sewers blast under them!

A sluggish creature
and difficult to house-train,
it spatters its own nest.

Dirty money gives dirty access.
And we were the generation
of positive disgrace.

And I want to throw my pen down.
And I want to throw my self down
and hang loose over some vault of peace.

Bright gulls, gracefully idling
in the blue and wholesome heights
above our aerials;

fatted magpie
big and bold
in the apple shade;

grey maggot, succulent
underfoot, inexorable
on your invisible way;

O green ash branches
whispering
against the sunny masonry;

Ah! baby spider
so swift
on the painted sill.

Fellow citizens! I embrace
your grasping manners, your natural behaviour,
as we thrive together for an instant.

And those also, friends and others,
of whose presences, deteriorating
here, there and elsewhere

I am acutely aware.
Here's a hug while the mood is on me.
Take your places around my table

one last time together.
Settling yourselves carefully,
startled you are on our list.

Uneasy. Delighted
if only there had been
a little more notice.

And let us not be bound by precedent.
We shall certainly need
an additional table or two.

The moment is at hand.
Take one another
and eat.

You, peremptory and commanding so long ago,
that so swiftly and methodically
discovered your limits.

You, so hesitant, so soon presumptuous,
urgent and confiding, breathing close
about nothing.

You, insistent, weak-smiling,
employing tedium to persuade,
vanishing when satisfied.

4

You, capering, predatory, inexhaustible
in ideas, the one thing certain
we will never know what was on your mind.

You with your bedtime mug of disappointment
—the loser in every struggle;
always on the right side.

You, flushed with bonhomie
but serious on the question of expenses;
always first with the bad news.

You, elbowing your way in,
out of your depth,
clumsy and comical, but determined;

surfacing long afterwards
in the Southern suburbs,
doing well, steering clear.

You, ageing in your junior grade,
applying your rules of thumb
with emphasis and ease.

You, managing the marginal cases
at your careworn desk.
Keeping the fees flowing.

And you, all smiles on the formal floor,
muscling past the ladies
to get at the archbishop;

dedicated and purposeful,
you silenced us
with your skills in analysis,

excited us
with your direct methods,
and were startled with us at the result.

You, in morose inadequacy,
settling your contemporaries in order of precedence,
denying what you still might: discern.

Discern process. You know that,
mangled by it. We are all participants
in a process that requires waste.

You that, with an ear
for the cold fathoms of the self,
whistled up the Song of our own Earth,

turned a spirit off the rocks
into a fire in the gut
and, in the final phase,

losing our first attention,
became an entertainer
among the lesser gentry.

You, our hectoring pontifical hack,
changing carthorses in midstream,
educating yourself in public.

You, our grocer's curate,
busy a long time in the back room,
suddenly up front grinning among the special offers.

And you, lecturing off the cuff, from on high,
the index cards arranged
behind the soles of your hands:

The procedures of criticism are understood.
Work not amenable to those procedures
does not call for consideration.

Ending with a modest bow
as though you had
said something.

Beware the assumption of authority,
the impulse to condescend,
especially when missing the point.

You, invoking a universal
commonsense about art
—not dismissing *Finnegans Wake*

but more interested in finding
an accessible medium that will work
for the general reader.

And you, handling the market direct,
tangled in your keys,
uproarious, but serious behind the fun,

an artist to your elbow tips.
Forgotten, your past master,
your training like an animal.

And you. Fiddler with the pale eyebrows
and the holy water for blood,
your fingers flying in the last movement.

But give us a kiss.
For we are going somewhere,
and need every scrap of good.

Though only of good.
A stiff midfinger in stern warning,
remembering one unnatural

saddled with a womb, to whom
the organic was intolerable;
one with a cast in her point of view;

and one hugging her grey stare in the morning,
stark staring sober,
waiting while her acid came to the boil.

And one, ascending by the three sisters,
appearing bodily
in my inward-staring grotto.

With an unhappy trinity
letting in the outer dark.
One, withered and erect, satisfied

that poetry is anything extruded in pentameter;
recalling his first Catholics with amusement
—Bernadette, Brendan,

                    Fergus, Cuchulainn . . .
Your views on the just society?
The eyes and the lips narrow.

One, swift-mounted, tight-hammed, commanding ham-fisted
at the inner table: We have it all together.
It looks good. The Blue Nun is on me.

An activist commentator descending on London
and the serious papers with his briefcase
full of applied literature

and a load of dirty linen
ironed across his arm;
balked in Redmondite bafflement

at human behaviour.
But writing so melodiously
you have to forgive him anything.

And remember we are dealing with the slow to learn,
whose fathers, wiping the blood up after yours,
fought the wrong Civil War.

That dream again. I am perched on a tank
in my pyjamas. I am pointing
toward Mullingar: *Secession is at an end.*

*

The world laid low
and the wind blew like a dust
Alexander, Caesar, and all their followers.

Tara is grass;
and look how it stands with Troy . . .
And we were the generation also of privilege,

to have seen the vitals of Empire tied off
in a knot of the cruel and comic.
Not to misunderstand

—the English are a fine people
in their proper place.
And two that circumstance saddled with each other

might have turned out something less like
the bully marriage next door
with the delph dancing off the wall

but the Creator's Anti-Christ was at Him.
A modest proposal:
everything West of the Shannon,

women and children included,
to be declared fair game.
Helicopters, rifles and night-glasses permitted.

The natives to have explosive
and ambush and man-trap privileges.
Unparallelled sport

and in the tradition
—the contemporary manifestation
of an evolving reality.

*

And he said,
Have love for one another
as I have loved the lot of you.

And now let us lift our thoughts
to our holy distracted Mother
torn between two stools.

Patroness of the manageable Catholic
that can twist on a threepenny bit;
and of the more difficult Protestant

twisting in the other direction
and interested more in property;
Thou that smilest however

on the pious of both persuasions
closest to the sources of supply,
guide us and save.

*

Enough.
That there is more spleen
than good sense in all of this, I admit

—and back to the Encyclopaedia I go.
Diderot, my hand upon it.
The pen writhed

and moved under my thumb
and dipped again
in its organic pot.

I

There are established personal places
that receive our lives' heat
and adapt in their mass, like stone.

These absorb in their changes
the radiance of change in us,
and give it back

to the darkness of our understanding,
directionless
into the returning cold.

Apostle of Hope

A greeting, and thanks, from this sick place
—our half-blind watch tower watching us
across the empty market square,
a squad of baby-looking troops
with deadly undernourished faces
waltzing across the cracked cement,
kneeling and posing with their guns.
Our polite faces packed with hate.

I won't forget your lair of a town.
That business breakfast there beside us,
the worried flashy expedients
for bringing life to the market centre.
At night, on our own, when the streets emptied,
the terrible number of waifs we met
in a silence of the stunned. The process
as it hath shown its waste to you.

Above all, lifted up on high,
enlarged by local enterprise,
Man the Measure cruciforked
upon His wheel, jacked up erect,
splayed like a target against the grey,
smooth as an ad. Grossness uprisen.
Godforsaken.
                    Forgive. Forgive.

The Impulse, ineradicable,
labours into life. Scrutiny;
manipulation toward some kind
of understanding; toward the Good.
The Process as it hath revealed
its Waste on high.
                    Let our hate reach that.

Seven

Will you dance at my doorway,
        perch at my porch?
Hurry darling,
        myriads in me demand it.

I flapped out haphazard
        across a glowing glade,
weightless, made of gauze,
        all the colours of the rainbow,

settled on a nodding
        solitary stem,
folded my wings
        and passed for a flower.

*

Foxglove and their faded flames nodded
down an alley of the greenwood shade.
A snapping fox shifted from doubt to doubt.

Steel carrion eyes
stared from a sharp midnight roof
above the empty square.

The leather claws
tightened on a stone face,
strengthening their hold with black nails.

*

Our thoughts touched in waking,
holding her live underarm,
honest hand on a tender tit.

A pigeon repeated its elaborate, brainless murmur.
The bedroom curtain inhaled
and filled with light.

A shadow of fumbled assent
with hand on uneasy heart,
in the fragrance of arm and throat.

*

In the name of the Father
all force

in the name of the spirit
gland of matter
blind staring bowel of being

in the name of the senses
ordered out
in their binary responding groves

deign, O crushed lips, pursed
in the woman dark
where'er you walk

to separate
beneath this kiss.

*

Seven.
A cloud shadow advanced
over the young barley

across the neighbouring fields,
and darkened the pair of cars
parked ill-matched in the yard.

Rituals of Departure

It is a misery, beloved friends, and my last wish.
But let us find what ease we can.
(Melancholy, retiring with her finger to our lips.)

*

We came out with the last suitcases strapped
and nothing left to say
onto the driveway under the high red oaks.

The children seen to and strapped in.
Speechless, and taking us by surprise
with their tears.

Our wagon turned away from the West.

*

And remember the detailed care you have had here.
And the love. And the other rituals of departure,
their ashes dying along our path.

Brothers in the Craft

In the creative generations there is often
a conspiracy of the mature and the brilliant young;
a taking in hand, in hopes of a handing on.

In the elder, an impulse against that settled state
when the elements work in balance against each other
in worn stability, no longer questioned;

to borrow something out of the restlessness
of the half ready, confide an ethereal itch
into new, committed fingers.

                    In the other,
a self-elect asking only to watch,
even be let hold something, the imbalance of growth.

These settle in the medium in their turn,
a part of the lasting colour of the work
drawn from the early accidental particulars.

Again and again, in the Fifties, 'we' attended
Austin Clarke. He murmured in mild malice
and directed his knife-glance curiously amongst us.

Out in the dark, on a tree branch near the Bridge,
the animus of Yeats perched.
                    Another part of the City,
Tonio Kroeger, malodorous, prowled Inchicore.

In Memory

I

You were silver-quiffed and tall
and smiling above us in public,
formal and at ease. Established.
Introducing I have forgotten what.

It is you I remember.
Authoritative, from the Department.
Published recently, and discussed.
Managing both careers.

The audience, mainly literary,
stood about, interested
in what was to come. But we
were gathered at your feet.

II

The years passed. Our group broke up.
The character of our generation
emerged, with the fulfilment
and the failure of early promise,

with achievement in surprising places,
and one startling success
revealing a sagacity and a scope
undreamed of at the time.

Some left the country, or disappeared
as though they had never been.
Others stayed in irregular contact
our conversations growing more general.

III

A few assembled lately
on a miserable occasion.
We found each other in a crowd
from the intervening years,

familiar and unfamiliar faces,
acquaintances and strangers,
friends from later interests.
An unpleasantness here and there

—one, quiet-spoken and confiding,
not to be trusted again;
one nursing an old dispute
and able behind the scenes.

The narrow face of envy.
Hardness of heart. Self.
False witness. The irreducible
malice and greed of the species.

*

We stood near the older trees
—your box, massive and pale,
waiting on a pile of clay.
With what you were taking with you.

And leaving. The memory
of a gentle self, affronted
by the unmanageable,
aroused and self-devouring.

I walked away, along a file
of long-established graves,
remembering our last meeting.
You, overcoated and withdrawn,

and sitting beside the fire
after another death.
Violent. One of yours,
inheriting your luck.

And I, making my way across
and settling at your side.
You starting a conversation
out of another time.

When I turned around to go back
it was a while before I discovered
our people among the others
—everybody everywhere with white hair.

Dura Mater

I

A potato smell came out from the kitchen door,
and a saucepan smell, with a piece of meat boiling.

She came along the passage in her slippers
with a fuzz of navy hair, and her long nails
held out wet out of the washing water.

Come here to me. Come here to me, my own son.

Stiff necked, she put up her pursed mouth
at her grown young—whatever idea she had of it
in the half-laugh and the bad temper in her eyes.

Will you look at him. How do you stick him at all.

And offered, and withdrew, a Cupid's Bow puckered,
closed lids, a cheek of withered silk,
the little smell of her hairline powdered over.

II

The withheld kiss returned
onto her stone forehead. Dura Mater.

To take it, a seal on her stone will,
in under the screwed lid.

III

He came out, stooping forward
with hands held down before him
still joined in the gesture of prayer,
his feet heavy but employed with care.

The sides of hair receding around his scalp
were moistened and dyed dark,
the face downcast,
the eyes soft but emphatic.

The air was filled with music.

*

He stepped into the funeral coach outside,
with quick irritated hand gestures
repeated without meaning,
a motiveless urging in the uplifted, inviting voice.

IV

I entered the lobby at the hour appointed,
a crowded place, low-ceilinged and obscure.
I found the place to wait, beside a great
illuminated plant in a stone pot.

Sudden and silent, he was there beside me.

I have come to speak with him, after so long,
because I have a question. But first to our places.
The instruments to hand on either side,
seated opposed, we settled down and ate.

I put the question. Certainly. Of course.
I am sorry you had to ask. There should be something
next week in the post, or the week after.
I'll see to that. And we must keep in touch.

Night Conference, Wood Quay: 6 June 1979

Our iron drum of timbers blazed and sparked
in rusty tatters at the mouth of the shed,
apples and bread and bottles of milk flickering.

'. . . We have a truce. They have made every mistake.
There are only a few thugs . . .' A voice rasped:
'You couldn't trust their oath.' A tired growl: hand-clapping.

The half-dug pits and night drains brimmed with matter.
A high hook hung from the dark: the swift crane locked
—and its steel spider brain—by our mental force.

*

Where are they, looking down. At what window.
Visages of rapine, outside our circle of light.
Their talk done. The white-cuffed marauders.

At the Western Ocean's Edge

Hero as liberator. There is also
the warrior marked by Fate, who overmasters
every enemy in the known world
until the elements reveal themselves.
And one, finding the foe inside his head,
who turned the struggle outward, against the sea.

Yeats discovered him through Lady Gregory,
and found him helpful as a second shadow
in his own sour duel with the middle classes.
He grew to know him well in his own right
—mental strife, renewal in reverse,
emotional response, the revelation.

Aogan O Rathaille felt their forces meeting
at the Western ocean's edge
—the energy of chaos and a shaping
counter-energy in throes of balance;
the gale wailing inland off the water
arousing a voice responding in his head,

storming back at the waves with their own force
in a posture of refusal, beggar rags
in tatters in a tempest of particulars.
A battered figure.
                          Any force remaining
held in waves of threat inside the mind.

As who can not confirm, that set his face
beyond the ninth shadow, into dead calm.
Dame Kindness, her bowels torn.
The stranger waiting on the steel horizon.

II

A Portrait of the Artist

We might have guessed it would end in argument
and the personal. The cool, acid exchanges
in the small hours, hoarse in the hall:
An architect is an artist! His first duty is beauty!
Finding our way down the steps;
walking up the terrace in relief.

A movement the other side of the Canal.
A pair of figures. . . .

*They had reached the canal bridge
and, turning from their course*

. . . continuing by the trees.
Locked in argument. About there.
One, nagging beauty to her place
among the senses. And the fool
lending a quick, inadequate ear:
But what is beauty.

My hands framed your throat in the night air.
A jewel of process.
                        The fugitive
held fast, exact in its accident

*

A car prowled across the Bridge
and halted, then turned in a slow curve
under the lamp back over the Canal
with another following on its track,
the tail lights pulsing rose.

A pair of shades. One, in a short skirt,
stirred herself; the other, in black leatherette,
held back against the railings,
the tip of her cigarette red. Her eyes
and her oyster mouth wet to my thoughts.

29

Administrator

We knew him first as a pious reputation,
businesslike, a new breed in the neighbourhood.
Stationed out among the people. Accustomed
to property and its management. Seldom seen.

He appeared once, in response to a complaint.
Entered the front hall, quietly discourteous,
suited in grey, easy to mistake
for a Protestant colleague;
and sat across the table, not really listening,
his response ready, looking past the speaker.

Our charges have certain needs. If these entail
annoyance for others that is unfortunate.
But we are there.
                    One lapse: a fumbled exit.

Then handed matters back to the lay staff.

Social Work

The meeting ended, and the delegates
moved off among themselves around the room.
I turned away to talk with a new neighbour.

A voice at my ear: 'I think we may give it up.'
A pair of furious Corporation officials
had stepped across to one of the high windows

with the social workers—the very Catholic doctor;
the house agent at his elbow, silver-haired—
and the parish priest, present as an observer.

The priest had chatted pleasantly before the meeting
but was otherwise quiet. He was speaking now
at the centre of the group, the others nodding.

The Stable

A loft, out of the market place,
of beams and whitened stone. Where the feed
was forked out, down to the Lane.

The ivy opposite, crept at last
over the date and initials painted
big and uneasy on the wall.
Where he kept the dray, half stacked with sacks.

O'Keeffe.
           Unbothered for forty years
he took the path from the stable door
back to the tap, and ran the water
into the bucket under his thumb.
And held the rim up spilling against
the teeth and the rubber lips of the horse
shifting its hooves in the wheaten stink.

Starting out, at the cross lane
it smelled the water off the Canal,
and fidgetted with a creak of straps
—tossing its face and rearing back
in the black tackle, half in earnest.
Then settled down between the shafts.

When O'Keeffe got sick
the wife and the helpful son-in-law
manoeuvred it out for the last time.
She waited back in the stable, crying.
They both knew well the kind of hold
they were handing over with the key.

When O'Keeffe came out his every move
was new and deliberate, exercising
along the Canal as far as the Lane
and back again by Haddington Road.

We sat in the kitchen across from each other:
I said Three Pounds. He made it Five.
We shook hands and I wrote it down
—the cash to be left on the window sill
where he left the rent.
                    And he wasn't gone
a month when the local roughs were in.

Household Spirits

From somewhere underneath my window
a thrush flew across to Comers' wall
and hovered under the dripping creeper,

holding its speckled brown body
agitated in the air, pecking up
at a little black bunch of berries,

then darted
back across the Lane
out of sight.

With the red juice in his mouth
he is consulting
the cannibal committee downstairs,

come at our call up through Australia
to stand carved in inquiry
or hang from their hooks and rafters;

mongrel images shaped in wood
with a fluency like dung.
Collect of innocent evils—

grinning nude with ibis,
a squat goose extruding a skull,
a scaled midget glaring,

a fatuous-ferocious flat head
on edge, like an animal pat,
no eyeball to no eyeball,
with muddied tongue outstuck.

The Bell

The bell on Haddington Road rang,
a fumbled clang behind the flats.
Anderson calling to his neighbour.

Hauling down on the high rope,
announcing his iron absolutes
audible in Inchicore.

Disturbing the sanctuary lamp
—cup of blood, seed of light,
hanging down from their dark height.

The Back Lane

The long workroom, in a faint light
    and a brain and book odour, as it was left.
The book I came for was still open

at the title-page and the sharp
    elderly down-tasting profile.
Close it with one finger, and gather it up.

             *

Outside, in the first night air,
    the double timber door scraped across
shut, under the wet vine.

I leaned back against the wood
    on serpent terms with Comers' cat
on the wall opposite, deadly in the open.

A black stain of new tar on the ground.
    Shade that in the beginning
moved upon the concrete.

And the remains of a cement mash
    emptied direct on the clay. Revealing
the clumsiness of the telephone people,

the slovenliness of the City and its lesser works.
    Culpable ignorance, distinguishing Man
from the cats and the other animals.

I stirred a half brain of cauliflower
    with my foot, on wet paper
against the corrugated tin and the neglect next door.

The Moon had set.
    And the Plough, emblem of toil.
And my own sign had descended.

Three Corporation lamps lit the way
    along the wall to the far corner.
And I started down the middle of the Lane

with the book at my heart
    and the pen patted in its pocket.
Past stables and back gates

in various use and ruin:
    vegetable and mongrel smells, a scent
of clay and roots and spinster flesh.

It was something to do with this
    brought me looking for you at this hour.
Not anything to do with management or method

—prejudice veiled as justice, and the particulars
    rearranged with a mathematical scowl;
or your direct childlike way with system.

But your shadow waiting
    and the hem of your skirt
catching on my own nettles and barbed wire.

The smell of exit:
    the next, and last, excitement.
My footsteps sounding dead among my neighbours.

With the simplest form, imposed
    —three lights brightening, embracing,
and fading into dark, at my own pace.

As far as your cross lane, City Fathers,
    and out among your larger works,
into the world of waste.

*

I stopped at the junction
in a first smell of water off the Canal,
and allowed myself a prayer with open arms:

the right arm held up hanging empty
and the left lifting my book;
with the wrists nailed back.

Lord, grant us a local watchfulness.
Accept us into that minority
driven toward a totality of response,

and I will lower these arms and embrace what I find.
—Embarrassed. Encountering my brother figure.
Startled likewise, in that posture

of seeming shyness, then glaring,
lips set and dark, hands down and averted
that have dipped in the same dish with mine.

But it was no one I knew,
hurrying out onto the terrace,
the features withdrawn and set in shame.

The Stranger

Years ago, while we were settling in,
I saw him passing by this side of the Canal,
a clerk from somewhere in the area.

Then, more accustomed to the neighbourhood,
I noticed him the other side of the Bridge,
crossing over from Mount Street opposite

or turning away in the dark along the base
of the heavy-set terrace, back around the Church
with the little peppercanister cupola.

One evening, when our house was full of neighbours
met in upset, I was standing by the drapes
and saw his face outside, turned up to the light.

And once in Baggot Street I was talking with someone
when he passed with a word or two to the other, his face
arab up close. We smiled in antipathy.

In another time I might have put it down
to evil luck or early death—the Stranger
close upon our heels—and taken care.

But you and I were starting to deal already
with troubles any Stranger might desire.
Our minds in their teeming patterns died each night.

Once, at an upper window, at my desk,
with the photographs and cuttings pinned in fury
around the wall, and tacked across the blind,

I found a structure for my mess of angers,
lifted out of the school dark:
                              Distracted

one morning by a stream, in circumstances
of loveliness and quiet, not for him,
a poet sank to the ground and hid his face

in harrowed sleep. A kindly beauty approached,
unworldly, but familiar—one of us—
comforted his misery, turned his thoughts

toward some theatrical hope . . . He reawakened
to the same tedium.
                              A simple form,

adjusted simply with the situation;
open to local application; weakened
by repetition; ridiculed and renewed

at last in parody. My pen quickened
in a pulse of doggerel ease.
                              When I beheld him

under the Moon, the other side of the road.
Overacting, bowing with respect,
resuming his night patrol along the terrace.

Leaving my fingers stopped above the paper.

Departure Platforms

A swan erected in anger, stiffening his neck.
His cygnets were busy, pecking and paddling
grey-furred among the heaps of worn tyres
around the sunny dock in Portobello
—the Canal harbour they filled in years ago.

A sack floated, half sunk, against the bank
where the people from the new Canal Hotel
stepped onto their fat, fashionable barges.

*

A crowd of people came hurrying up the staircase.

A girl with thick spectacles entered
and looked around her, one leg kneeling
in a metal thing, turning back and forth
with practised movements. 'A knee-crutch', I whispered.

A woman stood a moment inside the gate
resting, in middle age, with a heavy suitcase,
her legs wrapped in reddened bandages.
'Look', I whispered. 'They are still bleeding.'

He laughed: 'They come to your call.'

The Last

Standing stone still on the path, with long pale chin
    under a broad-brimmed hat, and aged eyes
staring down Baggot Street across his stick.
    Jack Yeats. The last.

Upright, stately and blind, and hesitating
    solitary on the lavatory floor
after the Government meeting down the hall.
    De Valera. The last.

Memory of W. H. Auden

A tangle of concerns
above the dark channel of Baggot Street.
Jesus in History. Man and his Symbols.
Civilization Surprised in her Underwear.

Lost—turning away toward something—
with my claws picking at the paint
on the sill at an upper window.

When I saw a stone-bright dead light
move on their scribal pallor.
Not an earthly effect. But not imagined,
the chimneys and the slate roofs South to the hills
touched by the same.
                    Swollen full
on high, a corpsegaze
imposed on a ghost of brilliance
staring down out of the Thirties
—rapt, radiant with vision and opinion,
flawed with the final furrows.
Secondary father, with cigarette.

Found—turning back into my den.
Your scarred regard bright on my shoulder,
my fingers finding their way
back about their business, with the taint upon them.

III

Better is an handful with quietness
than both hands full
with travail and vexation of spirit.

Better to leave now, and no more of this loving upset,
hate staining the door-jamb from a head possessed
—all things settled sour in their place,
my blind fingers forsaking your face.

Yet worst is the fool that foldeth his hands
and eateth his own flesh.

Madonna

Her high heels sounded nearer
in the aisle, tapping on the tiles.

She knelt beside me at the money-box
in the light of the candles,
under the Body with the woman feet.

Her head bowed. Her meat sweet.

*

She was busy, minding her hair
at the window, a long brushful held out.

Looking out at the night
and the light coming in
dead white off the street, and the shadow
invading our urinary privacy.

*

In concern and familiarity
it is done: our two awarenesses
narrowed into one point,
our piercing presences exchanged
in pleasantry and fright.

Our senses tired
and turning toward sleep,
our thoughts disordered
and lapped in fur,

your shoulder sleeping
distinct in my hand,
the tally of our encounters
reduced by one.

*

Cut and fold it open,
the thick orange, honey-coarse.
First blood: a saturated essence
tasted between the teeth.

I held the kettle out high
and emptied it
with a shrivelled hiss
boiling into the scalded pot.

A stubborn memory:
her tender, deliberate incursions.

Morning Coffee

I

We thought at first it was a body
rolling up with a blank belly onto the beach
the year our first-born babies died.

A big white earthenware vessel
settled staring up
open mouthed at us.

The first few who reached it
said they thought they caught
a smell of blood and milk.

Soon we were making up stories
about the First People
and telling them to our second born.

*

A loving little boy
        appeared on angel's wings
and showed his empty quiver.
        I filled it out of mine.

He vanished, but remembered:
        every dart
returning furious
        to my heart.

*

At a well beside the way
I alighted and put down
my lips to the water.

You, lifting your face
like a thirsty thing to mine,
I think I know you well:

of character retiring,
settled in your habits,
careful of your appearance;

with eyes open inward;
restless in disposition;
best left alone.

What matter if you seem
assured in your purpose
and animal commitment

but vague in direction
and effect on affairs?
Resolved on perfection

but soon indecisive?
We are all only pilgrims.
Travelling the night.

II

It was late in the morning dark,
at a side table,
the cup hot in my two hands,

my notes against the chair
with a few late cases
arguing among themselves.

A number of others were sitting
here and there around the long room.
One or two on each others' minds.

Outside, through the basement window,
there were feet hurrying, at eye height
around the corner, through the rain;

the cobbles opening in a wide yard
out among the old buildings
—the one shop, the offices

up the tenement stone stairs—
then closing in a lane by the Library
toward the car, still cooling.

I felt at my throat with thumb and finger.
The shaved leather. An hour earlier
—standing stripped at the sink,

holding the affected wrist
too long under the scalding tap,
sharp with pain and pleasure.

I pushed the chair back. The others
starting to wonder upstairs.
And left my cup for the woman waiting.

Visiting Hour

The pale inner left arm pierced and withdrawn.
A sweat-heated pillow flattened under my neck,
    I lay and fingered my mental parts.

A draft stirred the red curtain: a figure
at the foot of the bed, observing like a brother.
    Not much trace of him before our trouble.

But I needed nothing there. They must be letting
anybody in. I lifted a ham
    in thoughtful ease. The curtain settled back.

My tablets, bitten to a flour,
melted in an aftertaste of coffee.
    Awareness turned inward: a memory echoing,

with the blood beating injected in the face;
an aura, with a ghost of pleasure,
    melted in the loins, under the heart.

And the rail at the foot of the bed was empty again.
I turned over toward the high Victorian window.
    And she was there, at the crimson drape,

one thin hand out, denying. The other
pulled the lace away from her pale thigh
    and the dark stocking with the darker border,

in the pale motherly places
—the sac of flesh and fervour where we met
    and nourished each other for a while.

Mother, fragile in the smell of woodbine
and standing in your white folds,
    taking refreshment at my well of illness,

accept me in your medicine dark
until I wake, rereading the lace curtain,
    and turn back to the nothing in the doorway.

At the Head Table

The air grew dark with anger
toward the close of the celebration.
But remembering his purpose
he kept an even temper

thinking: I have devoted
my life, my entire career,
to the avoidance of affectation,
the way of entertainment

or the specialist response.
With always the same outcome.
Dislike. Misunderstanding.
But I will do what I can.

He rose, adjusted his garments,
lifted the lovely beaker
with the slim amphibian handles,
and turned to the source of trouble.

'Madam. Your health. Your patience.
Unlock those furious arms,
or we who respect and love you
will have to take offence.

How often, like this evening,
we have sat and watched it happen.
Discussing the same subjects
from our settled points of view,

our cheer turning to bitterness
with one careless word,
and then the loaded silence,
staring straight ahead.

O for the simple wisdom
to learn by our experience!
I know from my daily labour
it is not too much to ask.

This lovely cup before us
—this piece before all others—
gave me the greatest trouble,
in impulse and idea

and management of material,
in all the fine requirements
that bring the craftsman's stoop.
Yet proved the most rewarding,

perfect for its purpose,
holding an ample portion
measured most exactly,
pouring precise and full.

A fit vessel also
for vital decoration.
These marks of waves and footsteps
somewhere by the sea

—in fact a web of order,
each mark accommodating
the shapes of all the others
with none at fault, or false;

a system of living images
making increased response
to each increased demand
in the eye of the beholder,

with a final full response
across the entire surface
—a total theme—presented
to a full intense regard:

Nine waves out, a ship
lying low in the water,
battered from a journey,
the waves lapping around it

marked with the faint detail
of all the perils past.
The first firm footprints
emerging from the ocean

and planted on the seashore;
the sand grains shifted,
marked with the faint detail
of perils still to come.

Nine steps inland
where the two worlds meet, or divide,
a well of pure water,
with the first prints fading.'

He poured her a long portion
of the best blood brandy,
and lifted the brimming beaker
to her motherly regard.

'Remembering the Father,
His insult when offended,
our proneness to offend,
we will drink to His absent shade.'

A smile, dry and lipless,
disturbed her stern features.
Her lean arms opened,
acknowledging her son.

He limped off leftward
topping up their glasses
along the head table,

and danced off downward
out among the others,
everyone in turn.

IV

From Stephen's Green I set my feet
contented into Grafton Street.

The walls obscured the sinking sun.
Warmth and certainty were gone.

Open Court

(a fragment)

> . . . their shades
restless, and a muffled roar
guides us to the very door.

Outside, the spirit of the place,
the bar light flickering on his face,
haunts the gutter, sways and stoops
in rapt abandon, dives and swoops
with bow and fiddle—living things—
and, double-stopping, sweeps the strings
with passionate inaccuracy.

Inside: an overcrowded sty,
maroon in tone. Disputing hordes
mingle on the naked boards.
A spotted mirror, vast in size
and framed in bottles, multiplies
their slow turmoil. A chilly glaze
coats the lofty walls. A haze
of smoky light obscures the bar
where some of the more particular
have turned their backs.
                    Three poets sprawl,
silent, minor, by the wall.
Locked in his private agony,
showing the yellow of his eye,
a ruined Arnold turns his face
snarling into empty space,
flecks of black about his lips.
Next, a ruined Auden slips
lower on the leather seat,
his tonsure sunken in defeat
—roused to fits and starts of life
by the distant shrilling of his wife.
Last, downcast and liquid-lipped,
umbrella handle moistly gripped
and staring inward, doomed and mild,
a ruined, speechless Oscar Wilde.

Standing apart, a group of two:
an ageing author passing through,
a giant bringing into town
an atmosphere of vague renown,
a female student, open-eyed,
held to his patriarchal side.
Once more, with slow authority,
he tells her how it came that he
was passed all day from hand to hand
by friends and brilliant strangers and,
stupefied from endless bars
and ever-changing private cars,
established insecurely here
before two flattened pints of beer.
He halts a moment, losing track.
His hand slips lower down her back.

Six or seven, more or less
connected with the daily press,
are gathered in the centre light
debating the subject for the night
—Drink and the High Creative Arts—
with a novelist from Northern parts
collecting data in the South.
With every word that leaves his mouth,
tiny, admiring, by his knee
a lecturer in history
agrees excited.
                        Off his beat
and growing feeble on his feet,
a civil servant holds his case
close in a desolate embrace:
once more passed over.
                        Young and lean
a new arrival on the scene,
bluff, direct, with candid eye,
agreeable, and keeping dry.
Balanced back upon his heels,
in from the provinces, he feels
at home at once, cuts short his chat,
polite, with the tragic bureaucrat,

and aims a grin across his head
at one that (he has heard it said)
writes leaders on the local news
and manages the book reviews.

*

A chorus of disgust draws all
attention toward the farther wall.
Hemmed in the thickest of the press,
arrayed in spattered sporting dress
and seized by total indignation,
shocked at his shameful situation,
rages ruined Anonymous.
'Is nothing ever serious?'
Students struggle for a place
with betting men before his face.
He showers with a scornful snort
Truth and Beauty on his court:
'God deliver me from you
good-for-nothing mocking crew
that only know to jeer at Joy.
When I was a growing boy
and bent my back in ditch and dung
it wasn't mockery that flung
my holy body down one day
in ecstacy upon the clay,
but Truth that ne'er obeyed the call
of witty intellectual
—the tragic thing that shames the jiber
and monthly magazine subscriber!'

With happy cheers the bar resounds:
'Phonies! Culchies! Dirty hounds!
But why are you so hard on *us*?
Forgive! Forgive! Anonymous!'

'I'm not in the unforgiving or
forgiving business any more,'
Anon replies. 'Accursed pity
I ever came to Dublin city,
packed my bag and left behind
the very source I came to find.
I'd more between my thumb and finger
any Summer night I'd linger
up against a wooden gate
in simple pleasure. Now, too late,
here in Hell I count the cost:
simple conviction that I lost
in bothering with Dublin's loud
self-magnifying, empty crowd.
And double foolishness to flatter,
by attack, what doesn't matter.
But Time heals all and will produce
the only answer: What's the use?'

*

An acolyte with aching bladder
exits down a weeping ladder.
A dwarf official, with a tray,
collects and jingles on his way,
jams a while inside a pen
of duffle-coated racing men,
drops his eyes and whispers low:
'Excuse me, ladies.'
                              Time to go.
The hands are touching half-past ten.
Last drinks are swiftly measured, then
the barman halts and, howling 'Please!',
reaches back and rasps his keys
across an iron grating—'Gents!'
A moment's hush: the air grows tense.
We lift our faces from the trough.
The house lights flicker on and off.
A consciousness of distant parts,
with resignation, fills our hearts.

63

Rising and starting on our way
with cries of sadness and dismay,
we exit, crowding toward a pair
of sighing barmen at the rere.
Two clerks in liberated sex
collapse across each others' necks.
Friends we had not seen before
struggle, joking, through the door
and mingle in the dirty lane.
The door is slammed; they draw the chain.
We feel the cold among the slops
of fish and meat and poultry shops,
shrug our shoulders, turn our backs
and face a line of bursting sacks.

Then start upon our different ways.
Someone, sick or singing, stays
bent or leaning by the wall,
mindless of our mocking call.
The back door opens, throws a ray
of smoky light across the way.
A man, with brush, behind our backs
sweeps our waste across our tracks,
wipes his feet and bolts the door
against us, and is seen no more.

The dark is kind, where day will bring
some dew-drenched, green, revolting thing . . .

Dream

Picture a stony desert, baked and still.

A creature scuffles among the rocks
and stops, harrying its own vitals.
Another figure stands still on one foot,
pulling its head down between its shoulders,
torn by a great extinct beak. Other shapes
are lying here and there in the dust.

A group of human figures makes an appearance,
some seemingly at home in the pitiless waste.
One of their number is smiling all around him.
With another, bolder than the rest,
he approaches the first two creatures,
misjudging their apparent preoccupation.
He is caught by the first and swallowed in an instant.
His companion is seized by the second as a support.
The others squat on their heels, watching and waiting,
opening their throats and wailing
with low voices.
                    The scene darkens.

Then brightens again. Three years—ten years—have passed.
The desert is full of voices, and blossoming.
A breeze ruffles a carpet of wild flowers.
The man-eater, in a ring of bones,
bares his yellow teeth. It is a smile.
He holds a bunch of coarse herbs up to his snout;
cassia, the purging flax.
                    The monopod,
decked in bittersweet from head to foot,
hops about, garrulous.
                    Most of the early group
have vanished. A few are lying still.
A hand—a voice—flutters among them vaguely.

Another group is gathering, exercising
new expressions and attitudes as they come,
in range from faded sneer to witless discovery.
The last I remember is a ring of these ghosts
surrounding the scene. One of them, seven feet tall,
prods at random with a shadowy stick.
There is some excitement in one corner,
but most of the ghosts are merely shaking their heads.

I left the road where a stile entered the wood,
the dry trees standing quiet in their own grain,
bare branches with sharp fingers out everywhere.

Faced suddenly with a mouse body
upside down, staring, on a patch of bark.
The shape small, the wings flat.

Meant only to be half seen
quick in the half light: little leather angel
falling everywhere, snapping at the invisible.

We sat face to face at the kitchen table
silent in the morning cold,
our bodies and body hair clean.

Outside, a faint coarse call
came from a throat high in the light.
Higher up over the valley
a coarse quiet throat-answer.

Our raven couple
flying together, up toward their place
on the high rock shoulder.

I have known the hissing assemblies.
The preference for the ease of the spurious
—the measured poses and stupidities.

On a fragrant slope descending into the fog
over our foul ascending city
I turned away in refusal,
and held a handful of high grass
sweet and grey to my face.

OXFORD POETS

Fleur Adcock

Moniza Alvi

Kamau Brathwaite

Joseph Brodsky

Basil Bunting

Daniela Crăsnaru

W. H. Davies

Michael Donaghy

Keith Douglas

D. J. Enright

Roy Fisher

Ivor Gurney

David Harsent

Gwen Harwood

Anthony Hecht

Zbigniew Herbert

Thomas Kinsella

Brad Leithauser

Derek Mahon

Jamie McKendrick

Sean O'Brien

Peter Porter

Craig Raine

Zsuzsa Rakovszky

Henry Reed

Christopher Reid

Stephen Romer

Carole Satyamurti

Peter Scupham

Jo Shapcott

Penelope Shuttle

Anne Stevenson

George Szirtes

Grete Tartler

Edward Thomas

Charles Tomlinson

Marina Tsvetaeva

Chris Wallace-Crabbe

Hugo Williams